Happy Dussehra

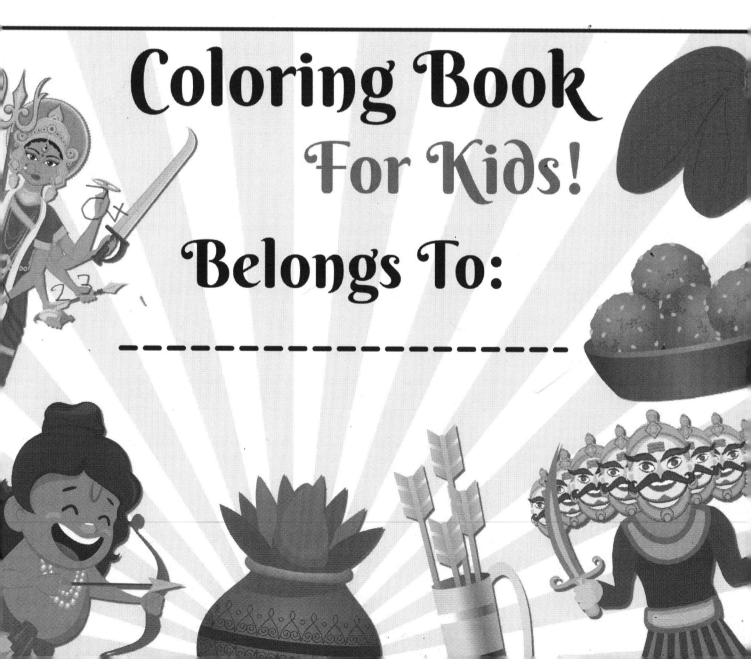

Coloring Book
For Kids!
Belongs To:

Title:Happy Dussehra Coloring Book For Kids

Author:Naomi Rover School

ISBN:9798476821496

TEST COLOR PAGE

Single-sided pages – every image is placed on its own black–backed page
to reduce the bleed-through problem found in other coloring books

HAPPY DUSSEHRA!

RAVANA

Single-sided pages - every image is placed on its own black-backed page
to reduce the bleed-through problem found in other coloring books

HAPPY DUSSEHRA!

RAMA

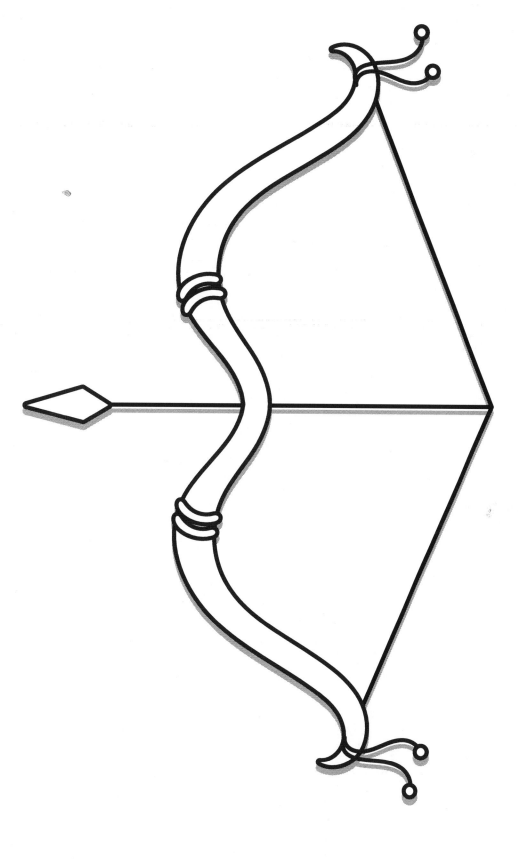

ARCH

Single-sided pages – every image is placed on its own black-backed page
to reduce the bleed-through problem found in other coloring books

HAPPY DUSSEHRA!

RASGULLA

Single-sided pages - every image is placed on its own black-backed page
to reduce the bleed-through problem found in other coloring books

HAPPY DUSSEHRA!

JALEBI

Single-sided pages - every image is placed on its own black-backed page
to reduce the bleed-through problem found in other coloring books

HAPPY DUSSEHRA!

LORD SHIVA

Single-sided pages - every image is placed on its own black-backed page
to reduce the bleed-through problem found in other coloring books

HAPPY DUSSEHRA!

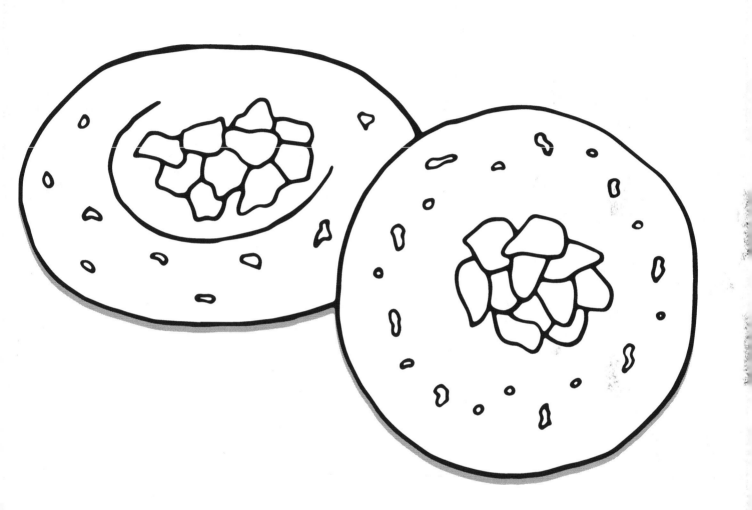

RASMALAI

Single-sided pages - every image is placed on its own black-backed page
to reduce the bleed-through problem found in other coloring books

HAPPY DUSSEHRA!

DURGA

HAPPY DUSSEHRA!

CURD

Single-sided pages - every image is placed on its own black-backed page
to reduce the bleed-through problem found in other coloring books

HAPPY DUSSEHRA!

Happy Dussehra!

DECORATIONS

Single-sided pages - every image is placed on its own black-backed page
to reduce the bleed-through problem found in other coloring books

HAPPY DUSSEHRA!

Single-sided pages - every image is placed on its own black-backed page
to reduce the bleed-through problem found in other coloring books

HAPPY DUSSEHRA!